Hearty Jalapeno Recipes

A Complete Cookbook of Dish Ideas
with HEAT!

Table of Contents

Introduction 4

There are plenty of breakfast recipes that include the spicy taste of jalapenos. It's a great way to wake up in the morning... 6

   1 – Jalapeno Breakfast Pie 7

   2 – Mexican Jalapeno Scrambled Eggs.....................9

   3 – Pumpkin & Jalapeno Breakfast Souffle 11

   4 – Jalapeno & Green Chili Breakfast Bake 14

   5 – Jalapeno Breakfast Quiche...........................16

Jalapenos lend themselves well to spicy recipes for lunch, dinner, side dishes and appetizers. Here are some great ones… 19

   6 – Cheesy Jalapeno Roll-Ups 20

   7 – Jalapeno Cornbread......................................22

   8 – Jalapeno Gazpacho......................................25

   9 – Stuffed Jalapenos with Sausage 28

   10 – Jalapeno Snackers......................................30

   11 – Slow Cooker Black Bean & Jalapeno Chili...................32

   12 – Mexican Corn with Jalapenos 35

   13 – Chicken Jalapeno Enchiladas 37

   14 – Honey Jalapeno Hummus...........................39

   15 – Macaroni & Cheese with Jalapenos 41

   16 – Ham & Jalapeno Hash 44

   17 – Creamy Jalapeno Chicken...........................46

   18 – Grilled Watermelon & Jalapenos 49

   19 – Jalapeno Cheeseburgers...........................51

   20 – Salmon with Jalapeno Strawberry Sauce 53

   21 – Chicken Nachos with Jalapenos 55

   22 – Jalapeno Asian Chicken.............................57

23 – Spicy, Sweet Jalapeno Poppers...................59

24 – Zoodles & Jalapeno Pesto 61

25 – Halibut Jalapeno Ceviche 63

Add some HEAT to your dessert with these jalapeno-infused sweets. Try some soon! 65

26 – Jalapeno Brownies...................................66

27 – Chocolate Chip Jalapeno Cookies...............69

28 – Apple & Jalapeno Pie 72

29 – Jalapeno Chocolate Spicy Cake 75

30 – Lime & Jalapeno Cheesecake....................78

Conclusion.. 81

Introduction

Aren't jalapeno peppers amazing? What makes them special? Jalapeno peppers are the ambassadors for spicy cuisine. If you master the use of jalapeno peppers, you can add unbelievable taste to your recipe repertoire. Having salsas made with jalapenos will open a wide range of dishes with HEAT just waiting for you to prepare and devour them.

If you've not purchased many jalapenos, they're usually next to their mild cousins, bell peppers, in the produce section of the supermarket. Select jalapenos that are taut and green. If they appear or feel mushy or wrinkled, they're a little past the prime time for cooking.

The part of chili peppers that gives them heat is capsaicin. It is more responsible for the spicy and unique flavors of dishes like many of those in Mexico. Once you know how to adjust the levels of capsaicin in your recipes, you can adjust the heat to your liking, and that of your family.

The seeds hold most of the capsaicin in the jalapeno. Scraping out the seeds and not using them gives you a milder recipe and less heat. Authentic Mexican and South American recipes are HOT because they typically leave the seeds in their recipes.

Actually, jalapenos only make it halfway up the list of the hottest peppers. The heat level also depends on the age of the pepper and the conditions in which it was grown.

So, fix your jalapeno dishes to appeal to you and your family, to get spicy flavor without making them too hot to enjoy. Turn the page – let's cook with jalapenos!

There are plenty of breakfast recipes that include the spicy taste of jalapenos. It's a great way to wake up in the morning...

1 – Jalapeno Breakfast Pie

This breakfast recipe is a bit sweet from the use of cinnamon, which presents a nice accent for the heat of the peppers. You can make the dish hotter by leaving out the cinnamon.

Makes 4 Servings

Cooking + Prep Time: 50 minutes

Ingredients:

- 4 to 6 chopped jalapeno peppers
- 6 eggs, large
- 2 cups of cheddar cheese, sharp

- 1 cup of bread crumbs, plain
- 1 tsp. of cinnamon, ground
- 1 tsp. of salt, kosher
- 1/2 tsp. of pepper, WHITE

Instructions:

1. Preheat the oven to 325F.

2. Add the chopped jalapenos to bottom of oiled casserole dish. Spread them evenly and sprinkle them with cheddar cheese.

3. Beat the eggs. Pour mixture over cheese.

4. Mix the bread crumbs with white pepper, salt and cinnamon. Evenly sprinkle on egg mixture.

5. Bake for 25-30 minutes, till browned lightly. Slice. Serve.

2 – Mexican Jalapeno Scrambled Eggs

This is a quick dish in the morning, made in the colors of the Mexican flag. It features green jalapenos, white onions & red tomatoes, the colors of the flag of Mexico. And it is SO tasty!

Makes 4-6 Servings

Cooking + Prep Time: 1/2 hour

Ingredients:

- 3 tbsp. of oil, canola
- 1 chopped small onion, white
- 1 stemmed, de-seeded, chopped jalapeno
- 1 cored, de-seeded, chopped plum tomato
- 2 tbsp. of cilantro leaves, sliced thinly
- Kosher salt & ground pepper, as desired
- 8 lightly beaten eggs, large

Instructions:

1. Heat the oil in 12" skillet on med-high. Add the tomato, onion and jalapeno. Season as desired. Stir while cooking for five to six minutes or so, till soft.

2. Add eggs and cilantro. Fold eggs over while cooking in large sized curds, till cooked completely through. Serve.

3 – Pumpkin & Jalapeno Breakfast Souffle

This souffle is airy and light, and perfect for breakfast. It's not at all hard to make, either. I use jalapenos ground into a powder in this recipe.

Makes 2-4 Servings

Cooking + Prep Time: 90 minutes

Ingredients:

- 2 tbsp. of butter, unsalted
- 2 tbsp. of flour, all-purpose

- 3/4 cup of milk, low fat
- 4 separated eggs, large
- 1 tsp. of chili powder
- 2 tsp. of jalapeno peppers, ground
- 1/2 cup of canned pureed pumpkin
- Optional: 1/4 tsp. of cloves, ground
- 1/2 tsp. of cinnamon, ground
- 1/2 tsp. of nutmeg, ground

Instructions:

1. Preheat the oven to 375F.

2. Heat large sized pan on med. heat. Add the butter, then the flour. Mix, forming a roux.

3. Add the milk. Stir till consistent. Then remove pan from the heat. Transfer to medium bowl.

4. Add to that bowl pumpkin, egg yolks and seasonings. Combine well.

5. In separate bowl, add the egg whites. Beat with hand mixer set on HIGH for five minutes or so, till whites become fluffy and are forming stiff peaks.

6. Fold egg whites GENTLY in small batches into roux-egg-pumpkin mixture.

7. Transfer mixture into large oiled casserole dish.

8. Bake for 20 to 30 minutes, till cooked completely through. Serve.

4 – Jalapeno & Green Chili Breakfast Bake

This breakfast bake can be as mild or hot as you'd like it to be. You can remove some of the jalapeno seeds or all of them, to balance the heat in your comfort zone.

Makes 2 Servings

Cooking + Prep Time: 45 minutes

Ingredients:

- 4 beaten eggs, large

- 1 splash milk, whole
- 1 chopped onion, small
- 1 x 4-ounce can of green chilies, fire roasted
- 3 de-seeded, scraped jalapeno peppers
- 1 cup of grated cheese, cheddar
- 1/4 cup of potato, grated
- 1 tsp. of seasoning, taco
- 1 tsp. of mustard
- For decoration: sliced tomato
- Sea salt & ground pepper, as desired

Instructions:

1. Lay the potato in bottom of casserole dish.

2. Beat the eggs in medium bowl. Add remaining ingredients.

3. Pour the egg mixture on top of potatoes. Decorate with tomato slices. Sprinkle the cheese over the top.

4. Bake for 30 to 40 minutes in 400F oven. Allow to set for five minutes. Serve.

5 – Jalapeno Breakfast Quiche

Here is a recipe that **Makes** breakfast fun! It can work for lunch, too. It's a morning quiche with a twist – jalapeno poppers.

Makes 6-8 Servings

Cooking + Prep Time: 1 & 1/2 hour

Ingredients:

- 11" quiche crust, pre-baked
- 4 oz. of softened cream cheese, reduced fat
- 4 chopped jalapeno peppers

- 1/2 cup of milk, 2%
- 1/2 cup of cream, heavy
- 5 eggs, large
- 1 tsp. of chili powder
- 2 cooked, chopped bacon slices
- 1/2 cup of shredded cheese, Mexican style
- Kosher salt & black, ground pepper, as desired

Instructions:

1. Preheat the oven to 350F.

2. Spread the cream cheese on the bottom of crust. Add jalapenos.

3. Heat sauce pan on med. heat and add the cream and milk. Bring to simmer. Reduce heat down to low.

4. Add eggs to large sized bowl. Add warmed cream and milk. Whisk well.

5. Add 1/2 bacon and chili powder. Season as desired and stir.

6. Pour the egg mixture into the pie crust. Bake for 1/2 hour.

7. Remove from the heat. Top with remaining bacon and cheese.

8. Bake for 10-12 minutes, till cheese has melted nicely.

9. Remove from the heat. Allow to cool a bit. Serve.

Jalapenos lend themselves well to spicy recipes for lunch, dinner, side dishes and appetizers. Here are some great ones...

6 – Cheesy Jalapeno Roll-Ups

These rolled-up tortilla bites are great for parties, and for side dishes at dinnertime, too. The mixture of green onions, cheese and sour cream, and the addition of jalapenos, all rolled into little tortillas, is SO tempting.

Makes 30 Servings

Cooking + Prep Time: 1 hour & 20 minutes

Ingredients:

- 1 cup of sour cream, reduced fat
- 1 x 8-oz. pkg. of softened cream cheese
- 1/2 cup of cheddar cheese shreds
- 3/4 cup of green onions, sliced
- 1 tbsp. of lime juice, fresh
- 1 tbsp. of jalapenos, de-seeded, minced
- 10 x 6" tortillas, flour
- 1 x 16-oz. jar of picante sauce

Instructions:

1. Mix the jalapeno peppers, lime juice, green onions, cheese, cream cheese and sour cream in medium sized bowl.

2. Spread 1 side of tortillas with mixture from step 1. Roll tortillas tightly. Place on serving dish. Cover with cling wrap. Place in refrigerator to chill for an hour or longer. Slice into 1" pieces and serve with the picante sauce.

7 – Jalapeno Cornbread

This golden cornbread is a pretty appetizer, with attractive flecks of red peppers and jalapenos. The mildly spicy flavor will be popular with almost everyone.

Makes 16 Servings

Cooking + Prep Time: 50 minutes

Ingredients:

- 1 & 1/2 cups of corn meal
- 1 tbsp. of flour, all-purpose
- 1 tbsp. of sugar, granulated
- 2 & 1/4 tsp. of baking powder

- 3/4 tsp. of salt, kosher
- 1/2 tsp. of baking soda
- 2 lightly beaten eggs, large
- 1 x 8 & 1/4-oz. can of corn, cream-style
- 1 cup of buttermilk
- 2/3 cup of oil, vegetable
- 2 cups of cheddar cheese shreds
- 1 chopped sweet red pepper, medium
- 1 de-seeded, diced jalapeno pepper
- 4-5 chopped green onions

Instructions:

1. Preheat oven to 350F.

2. Combine corn meal, sugar, flour, baking powder, baking soda and salt in large sized bowl. Set it aside.

3. Combine oil, buttermilk, corn and eggs in small sized bowl. Stir into bowl of dry ingredients till barely blended. Fold in onions, cheese and peppers.

4. Pour mixture in lightly greased 9x13-inch casserole dish. Bake in 350F oven for 30 to 35 minutes, till toothpick in

center comes back clean. Slice in squares and serve while warm.

8 – Jalapeno Gazpacho

This recipe tastes best if you are using some super-sweet, end of summertime tomatoes. Once you add the jalapenos, you'll find it to be the best gazpacho you've ever had.

Makes 6 Servings

Cooking + Prep Time: 2 hours & 50 minutes

Ingredients:

- 4 peeled, diced large tomatoes, fresh
- 1/2 peeled, diced English cucumber
- 1/2 cup of bell pepper, red, diced finely

- 1/4 cup of green onion, minced
- 1 de-seeded, minced large jalapeno
- 2 minced garlic cloves
- 1 tsp. of salt, kosher
- 1/2 tsp. of cumin, ground
- A pinch of oregano, dried
- 1 pinch of pepper, cayenne, +/- as desired
- 1 pint of tomatoes, cherry
- 1/4 cup of oil, olive
- 1 fresh lime, juice only
- 1 tbsp. of vinegar, balsamic
- 1 tsp. of Worcestershire sauce
- Kosher salt & ground pepper, as desired
- 2 tbsp. of fresh basil, sliced thinly

Instructions:

1. Combine the cucumber, tomatoes, green onion, bell pepper, garlic and jalapeno in large sized bowl. Add and stir ground pepper, oregano, cumin, salt and cayenne pepper.

2. Place Worcestershire sauce, vinegar, lime juice, olive oil and cherry tomatoes in food processor. Cover. Puree till you have a smooth mixture. Pour through strainer into cucumber/tomato mixture and combine well.

3. Place 1/3 of tomato mixture in food processor. Cover and puree till it has a smooth texture. Return the pureed mixture to the rest of the cucumber/tomato mixture and combine well. Cover. Place in refrigerator to chill for two hours.

4. Season the cold soup as desired. Ladle in bowls. Top with basil and serve.

9 – Stuffed Jalapenos with Sausage

Do you like dishes that pack an extra bit of heat? Then you will love these jalapenos stuffed with cheese and sausage. It's a great recipe for parties and get-togethers.

Makes 22 stuffed jalapenos (44 halved)

Cooking + Prep Time: 40 minutes

Ingredients:

- 1 lb. of pork sausage, bulk
- 1 x 8-oz. pkg. of softened cream cheese
- 1 cup of Parmesan cheese shreds

- 22 lengthways halved & de-seeded jalapeno peppers, large
- Optional: ranch dressing

Instructions:

1. Cook sausage on med. heat in large sized skillet till it is not pink anymore. Drain sausage.

2. Combine Parmesan and cream cheeses in small sized bowl and fold in the cooked sausage.

3. Spoon 1 tbsp. of mixture into jalapeno halves. Place in ungreased baking pans. Leave uncovered and bake in 425F oven for 15 to 20 minutes, till the filling has turned bubbly and peppers are browned lightly. Serve.

10 – Jalapeno Snackers

These are SO delicious. We don't enjoy a lot of SUPER spicy food, so I soak the de-seeded, sliced jalapenos in ice water for a couple hours and it takes out some of their heat.

Makes 10 Servings

Cooking + Prep Time: 40 minutes

Ingredients:

- 1 x 8-oz. pkg. of softened cream cheese
- 1 cup of cheddar cheese shreds
- 1/4 cup of mayonnaise
- 1 x 1-oz. pkg. of ranch dressing mix, dry
- 1 & 1/2 tsp. of garlic powder

- 20 halved, de-seeded jalapeno peppers, large
- 1 lb. of bacon, sliced, halved

Instructions:

1. Preheat oven to 400F.

2. Stir mayonnaise, cheddar cheese, cream cheese, garlic powder and ranch dressing mix in large bowl till blended evenly.

3. Spoon some of this mixture in each 1/2 jalapeno. Wrap with 1/2 bacon strip. Secure it with toothpick. Arrange wrapped halved jalapenos on broiler pan.

4. Bake at 400F till bacon isn't pink anymore and is starting to brown. This usually takes 15-20 minutes or so. Remove and serve.

11 – Slow Cooker Black Bean & Jalapeno Chili

Chili is an all-time favorite in our house. This inventive recipe takes that chili to another level. It changes up some of the flavors and adds that surprise, jalapenos.

Makes 16 Servings

Cooking + Prep Time: 25 minutes + 6 hours slow cooker time

Ingredients:

- 1 lb. of pork sausage, spicy, bulk, uncooked
- 1 chopped onion, large
- 2 chopped poblano peppers
- 2 de-seeded, chopped jalapeno peppers
- 3 tbsp. of tomato paste, low sodium
- 3 peeled, cubed sweet potatoes, large
- 4 x 14 & 1/2-oz. cans of undrained diced tomatoes, fire-roasted
- 2 x 15-oz. cans of rinsed, drained black beans
- 2 cups of stock, beef
- 2 tbsp. of chili powder
- 1 tbsp. of oregano, dried
- 1 tbsp. of coriander, ground
- 1 tbsp. of cumin, ground
- 1 tbsp. of paprika, smoked
- 1/4 cup of lime juice, fresh if possible
- For topping: queso fresco crumbles, chopped jalapenos & chopped red onion

Instructions:

1. In large sized skillet, stir while cooking sausage, jalapenos and poblanos on med. heat for eight to 10 minutes till the sausage has cooked fully. Transfer mixture to large slow cooker.

2. Add and stir tomato paste. Add tomatoes, sweet potatoes, stock, beans and spices. Combine by stirring.

3. Cover slow cooker. Cook on the LOW setting for six to seven hours, till sweet potatoes have become tender. Add and stir lime juice. Top with queso fresco crumbles, chopped jalapenos & chopped red onion. Serve.

12 – Mexican Corn with Jalapenos

This recipe came to our family by way of a relative in southern Texas. They like their foods HOT down there. We make it a bit milder than they do, and everyone requests this dish for BBQ's and holidays.

Makes 6 Servings

Cooking + Prep Time: 25 minutes

Ingredients:

- 2 x 15 & 1/4-oz. cans of drained whole kernel corn
- 1 x 8-oz. pkg. of cream cheese, reduced fat
- 1/4 cup of butter, unsalted
- 10 chopped jalapeno peppers
- 1 tsp. of garlic salt

Instructions:

1. Combine the cream cheese, corn, butter, garlic salt and jalapeno peppers in medium sized sauce pan.

2. Cook on med. heat for 10-12 minutes, till heated fully. Stir constantly after the cream cheese has started melting. Remove to bowls and serve.

13 – Chicken Jalapeno Enchiladas

These enchiladas are so creamy, and they will probably be popular for dinners and outings. Every time I make them for a gathering, I always get asked for the recipe.

Makes 10 Servings

Cooking + Prep Time: 1 & 1/4 hour

Ingredients:

- 2 x 15-oz. cans of tomato sauce, reduced sodium
- 4 x 10 & 3/4-oz. cans of undiluted condensed soup, cream of chicken
- 4 cups of sour cream, light
- 4 de-seeded, chopped jalapeno peppers

- 1 tsp. of salt, onion
- 1/4 tsp. of pepper, ground
- 4 cups of cubed chicken, cooked
- 3 cups of cheddar cheese shreds
- 20 x 8-inch tortillas, flour, warmed

Instructions:

1. Spread tomato sauce evenly into two lightly greased 9x13-inch casserole dishes. Set them aside.

2. Combine soup, jalapenos, sour cream, onion salt & ground pepper in large sized bowl. Add chicken and 2 cups of cheese.

3. Spread 1/2 cup of the chicken mixture down middle of all tortillas. Roll them up. Place seams facing down in casserole dishes. Top with the rest of the tomato sauce and sprinkle with last of the cheese.

4. Cover & bake one of the casseroles for 30-45 minutes at 350F till edges become bubbly. Remove and serve.

5. Cover remaining casserole and freeze for another meal.

14 – Honey Jalapeno Hummus

This hummus is SO tasty! I use roasted jalapenos and plenty of honey. I soak the jalapenos in ice water, too, to make the hummus milder. It's still flavorful and creamy.

Makes 4 Servings

Cooking + Prep Time: 20 minutes

Ingredients:

- 1 de-seeded, roasted jalapeno pepper

- 1 & 1/2 cups of chick peas, canned, rinsed & drained
- 1/4 cup of tahini
- 2 tbsp. of honey, organic
- 1/3 cup of oil, olive
- 1/4 tsp. of salt, kosher
- 1/4 tsp. of pepper, black, ground
- 3 tbsp. of water, iced
- Tortilla chips, bagged

Instructions:

1. Add chick peas to food processor. Blend till almost pureed. Add honey, jalapeno and tahini. Blend for another couple of minutes till ingredients have combined well.

2. Stream in oil with food processor continuing to run. Blend till you have smooth hummus.

3. Add kosher salt & ground pepper and blend again. Taste. Season as desired.

4. Stream in ice water with processor still running. Blend till mixture is once again smooth. Serve with tortilla chips.

15 – Macaroni & Cheese with Jalapenos

What could be better than a casserole dish of macaroni and cheese? Well, adding jalapenos certainly gives it a taste with HEAT. It's a great twist on traditional mac & cheese.

Makes 15 Servings

Cooking + Prep Time: 3 & 1/2 hours

Ingredients:

- 1 x 16-oz. pkg. of elbow macaroni, uncooked
- 6 tbsp. of butter, unsalted
- 4 de-seeded, chopped jalapeno peppers
- 3 cups of cheddar cheese shreds
- 2 cups of Colby-Jack cheese shreds
- 2 cups of milk, whole
- 1 x 10 & 3/4-oz. can of undiluted condensed soup, cream of onion
- 1 x 10 & 3/4-oz. can of undiluted condensed soup, cheddar cheese
- 1/2 cup of mayonnaise
- 1/4 tsp. of pepper, ground
- 1 cup of Ritz crackers, crushed

Instructions:

1. Cook the macaroni using instructions on package and drain. Then transfer to lightly greased large slow cooker.

2. Melt 2 tbsp. of butter in large sized skillet on med-high. Add the jalapeno peppers. Stir till tender but crisp. Add them to the slow cooker.

3. Add to slow cooker and stir mayonnaise, soups, milk, cheese and ground pepper.

4. Cover. Cook on the LOW setting till cheese has melted and the mixture has been heated fully through. This usually takes about three hours.

5. Melt remaining butter and stir in crumbled crackers. Sprinkle this mixture over slow cooker. Serve hot.

16 – Ham & Jalapeno Hash

Have some leftover ham to use up? If not, then buy some ham. This is an easy recipe to prepare with the sultry spice of jalapenos and smoked paprika. It's ready in 35 minutes or less.

Makes 6-8 Servings

Cooking + Prep Time: 1/2 hour

Ingredients:

- 1 & 1/2 tbsp. + 1 tbsp. of oil, olive
- 3/4 cup of chopped onion, red
- 2 tsp. of diced cloves of garlic
- 1/4 cup of de-seeded, diced jalapeno pepper, fresh

- 2 cups of scrubbed, cubed potatoes
- 2 & 1/2 cups of chopped ham
- 1/4 to 1/2 tsp. of paprika, smoked
- For garnishing: 2 to 3 tbsp. of cilantro, chopped

Instructions:

1. Heat 1 & 1/2 tbsp. of oil in heavy skillet on med-high. Add jalapeno, onion and garlic. Sauté till onions start turning translucent. Remove veggies from the skillet and set them aside.

2. Add the extra tbsp. of oil to skillet. Add potatoes and stir occasionally, allowing potatoes to cook till firm but not till crunchy. Don't stir constantly – the potatoes need to form a crust that is crispy.

3. Add ham to skillet with potatoes. Stir and combine. Heat ham. Add back jalapeno, onion and garlic and add hot paprika, as well. Stir and combine well. Warm mixture evenly. Garnish with cilantro and serve.

17 – Creamy Jalapeno Chicken

Here is a recipe that will make those traditional chicken breasts more interesting. The sauce is simply wonderful, and they go together so well.

Makes 4 Servings

Cooking + Prep Time: 1/2 hour

Ingredients:

- 4 x 4-oz. chicken breast halves, skinless, boneless
- 1/4 tsp. of salt, kosher
- 1 tbsp. of oil, canola
- 2 medium chopped onions
- 1/2 cup of chicken broth, reduced sodium
- 2 de-seeded, minced jalapeno peppers
- 2 tsp. of cumin, ground
- 3 oz. of cubed cream cheese, low fat
- 1/4 cup of sour cream, reduced fat
- 3 de-seeded, chopped tomatoes, plum
- 2 cups of hot rice, cooked

Instructions:

1. Sprinkle the chicken with kosher salt. Brown it on each side in canola oil in large skillet on med-high.

2. Add broth, onions, cumin and jalapenos. Bring to boil. Reduce the heat, then cover skillet. Simmer for five to seven minutes. Remove the chicken and keep it warm.

3. Stir in the sour cream and cream cheese with onion mixture and blend well. Add tomatoes and heat them through. Serve with the cooked rice and chicken.

18 – Grilled Watermelon & Jalapenos

This watermelon is prepared with only a bit of smoked salt. It gives it a campfire taste. Adding the grilled jalapenos **Makes** it HEAT heaven.

Makes 6 Servings

Cooking + Prep Time: 1/2 hour

Ingredients:

- For grill coating: oil, olive
- Watermelon, cut in triangles
- Jalapeno peppers
- Salt, smoked

Instructions:

1. Heat grill to 350F. Make sure grill is cleaned. Oil the grill, as well.

2. Place prepared peppers on grill. Close lid. Cook for three minutes per side till they blister. Remove them and let them cool a bit. Slice into rings.

3. Place triangles of watermelon on grill. Sprinkle with a bit of the smoked salt, not much at all.

4. Grill watermelon for 1 & 1/2 – 2 minutes, forming grill marks. Turn the triangles over. Grill them on other side. Salt one side only. Remove from the grill. Serve with the sliced jalapeno peppers.

19 – Jalapeno Cheeseburgers

Mexican and Latin American dishes influence the cuisine of other countries. Many people enjoy spicy foods because of that. Swiss cheese has a mellow flavor that lowers the heat level of the jalapenos used.

Makes 4 Servings

Cooking + Prep Time: 35 minutes

Ingredients:

- 2 lbs. of beef, ground
- 4 Swiss cheese slices

- 1 chopped onion, small
- 2-3 de-seeded, chopped jalapeno peppers, pickled
- 4 split, toasted hamburger buns
- Optional: ketchup and leaves of lettuce

Instructions:

1. Shape the beef into eight patties. Top four of them with cheese, jalapenos and onions. Top with other four patties and seal together by pressing the edges.

2. Place burgers on the grill and cover. Grill on med. heat for eight to nine minutes per side, till temperature is 160F and the juices are running clear.

3. Place burgers on buns. Top with lettuce and ketchup, as desired. Serve.

20 – Salmon with Jalapeno Strawberry Sauce

Salmon right off the grill bathed in jalapeno strawberry sauce will be a favorite dinner, especially during the summer months. The salmon is hearty, and the sauce is only slightly spicy.

Makes 4 Servings

Cooking + Prep Time: 20 minutes

Ingredients:

- 4 fillets of salmon
- Salt, kosher & pepper, ground, as desired
- Strawberry Jalapeno Sauce, bottled

Instructions:

1. Preheat your grill to med-high. Oil grates.

2. Season salmon as desired.

3. Place salmon on grill. Grill for three to four minutes per side, or till they are done to your liking. Top salmon with sauce and serve.

21 – Chicken Nachos with Jalapenos

This Mexican casserole is made with jalapenos, chicken and Doritos™. If you take it to a potluck, you're almost guaranteed not to be taking any leftovers home.

Makes 10 Servings

Cooking + Prep Time: 50 minutes

Ingredients:

- 4 cups of cooked chicken, cubed
- 1 lb. of cubed Velveeta™ cheese

- 2 x 10 & 3/4-oz. cans of undiluted, condensed soup, cream of chicken
- 1 x 10-oz. can of undrained diced tomatoes with the green chilies
- 1 cup of onion, chopped
- 1/2 tsp. of salt, garlic
- 1/4 tsp. of pepper, ground
- 1 x 14 & 1/2-oz. pkg. of tortilla chips, nacho cheese
- To serve: diced tomatoes and sliced jalapenos

Instructions:

1. Mix the first seven ingredients in large bowl and mix them well. Crush the chips and set one cup aside for topping. Add the rest of the chips to your chicken mixture.

2. Spoon mixture into lightly greased 9x13-inch casserole dish. Sprinkle with the reserved chips.

3. Leave dish uncovered. Bake on 350F till the cheese has melted and edges are bubbling. Remove from oven and top with sliced jalapenos and diced tomatoes. Serve.

22 – Jalapeno Asian Chicken

This dish offers you spicy, sweet and savory goodness in a meal that is super easy to make. The chicken doesn't need to be breaded or fried, and the honey lemon sauce rocks.

Makes 4 Servings

Cooking + Prep Time: 25 minutes

Ingredients:

- 1 tbsp. of oil, vegetable
- 1 lb. of 1" cubed chicken breasts, skinless, boneless
- Kosher salt & ground pepper, black
- 2 tbsp. of chopped cilantro leaves, fresh
- 1/2 tsp. of sesame seeds
- 1 sliced jalapeno

Lemon Honey Vinaigrette sauce, bottled

Instructions:

1. Heat the oil in large sized skillet on med-high. Season the chicken as desired. Add the chicken to skillet. Cook for two to three minutes, till golden. Set it aside.

2. Add the lemon and honey sauce. Garnish with cilantro and sesame seeds as desired and serve promptly.

23 – Spicy, Sweet Jalapeno Poppers

Start a party fast with jalapeno poppers. You can make them the day before and then just bake them before you serve them.

Makes 12 Servings

Cooking + Prep Time: 35 minutes

Ingredients:

- 6 medium jalapeno peppers, de-seeded, halved
- 4 oz. of softened cream cheese, reduced fat
- 2 tbsp. of cheddar cheese shreds

- 6 width-wise halved slices of bacon
- 1/4 cup of brown sugar, packed
- 1 tbsp. of seasoning mix, chili

Instructions:

1. Slice jalapeno peppers in lengthways halves. Remove the seeds. Beat the cheeses in small sized bowl till they are blended well. Spoon the mixture into the halved peppers. Wrap 1/2 slice bacon around halves.

2. Combine the chili seasoning with the brown sugar. Coat the peppers with this mixture. Place in lightly greased 10"x15"x1" baking pan.

3. Next, bake poppers at 350F till bacon has firmed up. This usually takes 15 to 20 minutes or so. Serve hot.

24 – Zoodles & Jalapeno Pesto

This pesto brings great taste to zucchini noodles, also known as "zoodles". Leftovers can be kept in your refrigerator for about a week.

Makes 4 Servings

Cooking + Prep Time: 35 minutes

Ingredients:

- 1/2 cup of walnuts, chopped
- 1 chopped garlic clove

- 1 de-seeded, then de-stemmed & chopped 2" jalapeno
- 1 cup of Asiago cheese, grated, + extra to serve
- 1 tsp. of salt, kosher
- 1/2 tsp. of pepper, ground, black
- 2 heaping full cups of spinach, baby
- 2 heaping full cups of arugula greens
- 1/2 cup of oil, olive
- 2 zucchinis, large
- To serve: chopped basil or parsley

Instructions:

1. Combine a cup of cheese, walnuts, jalapeno, garlic, kosher salt & ground pepper. Process till ground finely.

2. Add arugula and spinach. Process till ground finely again. Leave motor of processor running and drizzle oil in slowly. Process till you have a smooth texture.

3. Use spiralizer or grater to shred zucchinis. Toss them with some pesto. Sprinkle with Asiago cheese and add basil or parsley. Serve.

25 – Halibut Jalapeno Ceviche

This ceviche is fresh and light. The jalapenos make it a more interesting dish to serve family and friends.

Makes 6 Servings

Cooking + Prep Time: 15 minutes + 10 minutes chilling time

Ingredients:

- 1 grated clove of garlic
- 3/4 cup of lime juice, fresh

- 1 tsp. of agave nectar
- 2 tbsp. of tequila blanco
- 1/4 cubed pineapple, small
- 1 chopped tomato, medium
- 1 chopped onion, small
- 4 trimmed and sliced radishes
- 1/2 sliced jalapeno
- 6 oz. of 1"-cubed fillet of halibut with bloodline, skin and bones removed
- 1 x 1/2" cubed avocado
- 1/4 cup of cilantro, chopped finely
- 1/4 cup of mint, chopped finely
- Salt, kosher

Instructions:

1. Mix the agave nectar, tequila, lime juice and garlic in large sized bowl. Add the halibut, jalapeno, radishes, onions, tomatoes and pineapple. Toss and coat well.

2. Fold in the mint, avocado and cilantro and season as desired. Chill for about 10 minutes and serve.

Add some HEAT to your dessert with these jalapeno-infused sweets. Try some soon!

26 – Jalapeno Brownies

These jalapeno brownies will really heat up dessert time at your house. They can be served with vanilla ice cream or whipped cream to cool them down a bit.

Makes 16 brownies

Cooking + Prep Time: 35 minutes

Ingredients:

- 1/2 cup of oil, olive
- 1 cup of sugar, granulated

- 2 eggs, large
- 1 pureed 4-oz. can of diced jalapenos
- 1 tsp. of vanilla extract, pure
- 1/2 cup plus 3 tbsp. of flour, all-purpose
- 1/3 cup of powdered cocoa
- 1/4 tsp. of baking powder

1/4 tsp. of salt, kosher

Instructions:

1. Preheat oven to 350F. Grease one 8" square baking pan.

2. Whisk flour, salt, cocoa powder and baking powder together in medium bowl till there aren't any cocoa clumps remaining.

3. In a separate bowl, whisk vanilla, jalapenos, eggs, sugar and oil together till combined well. Add dry mixture. Stir till barely combined.

4. Pour batter in prepared pan. Level the top.

5. Bake for 15-20 minutes, till brownies are pulling away from sides of pan.

6. Allow to completely cool in pan on wire rack. Cut and serve.

27 – Chocolate Chip Jalapeno Cookies

Chocolate and jalapenos cooked together are a treat that many people have never experienced. The peppers have heat that will intensify chocolate. They're a great combination!

Makes 60 cookies

Cooking + Prep Time: 20 minutes

Ingredients:

- 1 & 1/2 sticks of room temp. butter, unsalted
- 3/4 cup of sugar, granulated

- 1/4 cup of brown sugar, dark, packed firmly
- 1 room temp. egg, large
- 1 & 1/2 tsp. of vanilla extract, pure
- 1 & 3/4 cups of flour, all-purpose
- 1/2 tsp. of baking soda
- 1/2 tsp. of salt, kosher
- 2 cups of semi-sweet chocolate chips
- 4 seeded and diced jalapenos, small

Instructions:

1. Preheat the oven to 350F.

2. Line the two cookie sheets with a baking paper and set them aside.

3. Sift baking soda, flour and kosher salt together in medium sized bowl. Set it aside.

4. Add the brown sugar, butter and granulated sugar to large sized bowl. Beat till it has a creamy texture. Beat in an egg till combined well. Beat vanilla in till combined well, too.

5. Add flour mixture slowly to sugar mixture till combined fully. Add and stir jalapeno peppers and chocolate chips.

6. Place heaping-tsp. sized blobs of dough on cookie sheet with two inches between them. Bake at 350F for eight to 10 minutes, till edges are browned lightly.

7. Remove cookies from oven. Let them cool on the cookie sheet for a couple minutes. Then place on rack to finish cooling. Serve.

8. Leftover cookies could be stored for up to one week or frozen for maximum of three months in sealed container.

28 – Apple & Jalapeno Pie

This is not the apple pie your grandma used to serve when you were young. It offers sugar and cinnamon for sweetness and a KICK of heat with the jalapenos.

Makes 6 Servings

Cooking + Prep Time: 1 hour

Ingredients:

- 1 x 14-ounce box of pie crust, refrigerated and set out to room temperature
- 2 tbsp. of pepper jelly, hot

- 6 cups of peeled, then cored & sliced apples, Granny Smith
- 2 tsp. of de-seeded, diced jalapeno pepper
- 3/4 cup of sugar, granulated
- 1/2 cup of brown sugar, packed
- 2 tbsp. of flour, all-purpose
- 3/4 tsp. of cinnamon, ground
- 1/8 tsp. of nutmeg, ground
- 1/4 tsp. of salt, kosher
- 1 tbsp. of lemon juice, fresh if available

Instructions:

1. Preheat oven to 425F. Sprinkle each side of one pie crust with all-purpose flour. Rub the flour over the whole side. Press crust into 9" ceramic or glass pie plate. Spread pepper jelly into bottom of crust and set the plate aside.

2. Add lemon juice, salt, nutmeg, cinnamon, flour, both sugars, jalapeno pepper and apples to large sized bowl. Stir till combined well. Pour this mixture in pie crust.

3. Roll out other pie crust so it will be extending 1/2" beyond pie plate rim. Place this crust on the top of pie. Tuck edge

under bottom crust edge. Seal by pressing together and crimp edges with fork or fingers.

4. Cut five x two-inch slits in top crust with sharp knife. They should run from middle out toward pie crust edge, so that steam will be able to escape easily.

5. Place foil on edge of pie crusts so they won't burn.

6. Bake pie on center shelf for 20-30 minutes. Remove foil. Bake for 8-10 more minutes, till you have a golden-brown crust.

7. Allow pie to sit for two hours or longer, to juices can be absorbed. Serve.

29 – Jalapeno Chocolate Spicy Cake

This cake is moist and fluffy, and simply amazing. The jalapenos don't overpower the cinnamon, and the buttercream frosting tops it off nicely.

Makes 10-12 Servings

Cooking + Prep Time: 1 & 1/2 hour

Ingredients:

- 1 cup of melted, cooled chocolate chips
- 1 & 1/4 cup of sugar, granulated
- 3/4 cup of softened butter, unsalted
- 1 tsp. of vanilla extract, pure
- 3 eggs, large
- 2 cups of flour, all-purpose
- 1 tbsp. of cinnamon, ground
- 2 tsp. of baking powder OR baking soda
- 1/2 tsp. of salt, kosher
- 1 cup of milk, whole
- 1 or 2 tbsp. of finely chopped jalapeno, canned
- Chocolate frosting, prepared

Instructions:

1. Preheat the oven to 350F. Grease 2 x 9" baking pans, round

2. Beat the vanilla, sugar and butter in large bowl on mixer. Add the eggs in and beat for about one minute. Beat in chocolate.

3. Combine the cinnamon, baking soda/powder, salt and flour. Beat this into the chocolate mixture along with milk. Stir in the jalapeno pieces. Pour the batter in baking pans.

4. Bake at 350F for 30 to 35 minutes. Toothpick inserted in center should come back clean. Allow to cool in the pans for 15-20 minutes. Invert on wire racks so they can finish cooling. Frost the cake, slice and serve.

30 – Lime & Jalapeno Cheesecake

This cheesecake was supposedly created by accident, when someone "dropped" a jalapeno into cheesecake batter. I think it was intentional, and the result is hot but sweet, and delicious.

Makes 8 Servings

Cooking + Prep Time: 1 & 3/4 hours + 4+ hours chilling time

Ingredients:

- 2 cups of crumbs, graham cracker
- 1/2 cup of melted butter, unsalted
- 3 x 8-oz. pkgs. of softened cream cheese
- 3/4 cup of sugar, granulated
- 3/4 cup of sour cream
- 3 room temp. eggs, large
- 1 tbsp. of flour, all-purpose
- 1 tsp. of vanilla extract, pure
- 1/2 cup of lime juice, fresh if available
- 1 seeded, minced jalapeno pepper

Instructions:

1. Preheat the oven to 375F.

2. Mix butter and cracker crumbs in large sized bowl till moistened evenly. Press this mixture into bottom of 9" spring-form pan.

3. Next, bake crust only at 375F till crust smells toasted and has browned lightly. Remove from oven. Set it aside so it can cool properly.

4. Beat sour cream, cream cheese and sugar in large bowl with electric mixer, till fluffy and light. Beat eggs into mixture, one after another.

5. Beat lime juice, flour and vanilla extract into mixture. Fold jalapeno into mixture, just sufficiently to mix evenly. Pour into prepared crust.

6. Bake at 375F for 15 minutes. Reduce heat down to 250F. Continue to bake till center is barely set. This usually takes 50-55 minutes or so.

7. Remove from oven. Allow to cool outside refrigerator for one hour. Then place in fridge and allow to cool for at least four hours, or overnight. Slice and serve.

Conclusion

This jalapeno cookbook has shown you...

How to use jalapeno peppers to affect unique and spicy tastes in dishes both well-known and rare.

How can you include jalapenos in your home recipes?

You can...

- Make jalapeno-enhanced breakfast dishes. They are tastier than you might have imagined, and not too hot, depending on whether you use the seeds or not.
- Learn to cook with ingredients that temper the taste of jalapenos. This allows you to use the spicy peppers in more types of dishes.
- Enjoy making delectable nacho dishes with jalapenos, including plain or flavored tortilla chips.
- Make dishes using chicken and cheeses, which are often used in cooking with jalapenos.

- Make various types of desserts like cheesecake and cookies, all blended with jalapenos, which will tempt your family's sweet tooth.

Have fun experimenting! Enjoy the results!

Printed in Poland
by Amazon Fulfillment
Poland Sp. z o.o., Wrocław

53454138R00047